Roblox Lua: Understandi~~ Basics

By Shane Merchant & Andi Muhaxheri
Edited by AxonMega

Introduction

Thank you for picking up *Roblox Lua: Understanding the Basics*. As you may have come to suspect, this book will be going over the basic ideas needed to begin programming using the Roblox platform.

We will be teaching you how to think and write like a programmer, so that you can begin to grasp the concepts of coming up with your own work(s).

Roblox Lua: Understanding the Basics will be the first of several books covering Roblox programming. Be sure to check out our next book, ***Roblox Lua: Programming Weapons***, where we will be teaching you how to program your own in-game tools such as weapons, and other player-held objects.

Table of Contents

Definitions

In case you don't understand something in a section, feel free to search for it here. If you still don't understand what something is, check **wiki.roblox.com** or **Google**!

Home - Studio tab that contains all basic components.

Model - Studio tab for using and editing parts.

Terrain - Studio tab that acts as a Terrain console. Used for making terrain.

Test - Studio tab that allows for testing your game in every way possible.

View - Studio tab for adding windows to your studio.

Plugins - Studio tab displaying all downloaded plugins.

Run - Runs your game in studio, but does not load in your avatar.

Play - Runs your game in a fake Studio-created server that spawns your avatar.

Collisions - A toggleable button under the *Home* tab. Allows parts to clip through each other when de-selected.

Anchor - Prevents objects in Studio from being affected by Roblox's physics.

Lobby - Spawn area, referred to as a *Lobby* on Roblox.

Map - The build that players actually play on in a game.

Script - A file containing your game's coding.

Scripting - The process of writing your code.

Part - The most basic of Roblox objects. Used for building.

Badge - An award players can earn in-game.

Game Pass - A pass players can buy to obtain special in-game abilities.

Backpack - Contains the player's gear.

Toolbox - Contains your models, decals, audios, meshes, etc. Also contains public free models, decals, audios, etc.

Output - Shows the status for your game's scripts when you select either Play or Run.

Explorer - A tab that shows every item inserted into a Roblox game.

Properties - A section that shows all of an object's properties.

GUI - Stands for *Graphical User Interface*; On-screen displays. (Home button, chat, etc)

Workspace - Explorer service that stores all of your game's active objects (Models, lobby, scripts).

Players - Explorer service that stores data for playing players.

Lighting - Explorer service that handles your game's lighting components.

ServerScriptService - Explorer service that contains your game's codes.

ServerStorage - Explorer service that contains your game's unused maps/buildings.

HttpService - Explorer service that handles request to external websites.

StarterGUI - Explorer service that contains user-created GUIs.

StarterPack - Explorer service that contains a user's gears and weapons.

CFrame - Data that represents an object's position and rotation.

Vector2 - Array of float values (X,Y)

Vector3 - Array of float values (X,Y,Z)

UDim - Stands for Universal Dimension, uses two coordinates. Consists of a Scale and Offset.

UDim2 - A data type made of two UDims. One for X coordinate and the other for Y. Used for positioning and scaling GUIs.

For Extra Guided Help

For extra help, Andi Muhaxheri (Co-Author of this book) has set up a playlist on YouTube.

These video tutorials are designed for you to follow along with as you're going through the book. This will boost your learning speed with Lua quite a bit!

There will ALSO be links to tutorial videos at the end of each and every section that we believe will help you get the drift of things.

You can also send us (the authors) a Direct Message on Twitter asking for help! We'd love to be of assistance!

@KinqAndiRBX (www.twitter.com/kinqandirbx) or @MerchantVIII (www.twitter.com/merchantviii)

http://bit.ly/2gl1iHR

Section 1: Starting up your Game

*The **first two Sections** will be going over the extreme basics. If you already know all about starting up games and getting around in Roblox Studio, please skip to **Section 3**.*

Section 1 Clause 1: Setting up your Game

Setting up your game is simple. Simply go to your game's page, select the 3 small horizontal squares at the top right, and select *Configure This Place*

Next, fill out the *Basic Settings*

Next, upload your own *Game Icon.* This is the picture that will appear on your profile, in your game favorites, on your recently played, and on the *Games* page. Game Icons are free to update.

Now, upload your own *Game Thumbnail.* This is the picture that will appear on your game's page. Thumbnails cost 10 Robux each. (Price may change)

Now, who do you want to have access to your game? What kind of players? Do you want to make players pay for the game before they enter? How many people would you prefer are in a server on your game? How many total players total can be playing in one server on your game? Do you want everyone to have access or just your friends? Do you only want Builders Club players playing? Do you want to sell VIP servers that players can buy at your game to play with their friends privately?

What kind of gear is allowed? Do you only want gears that match your game's genre to be allowed in? What kinds of gear types are allowed? What kind of chat do you want? Do you want the game copylocked? (makes it so players can't copy your game) do you want to allow comments? Does your game change the player's outfit?
Did you mess up on something in your game that you saved? Don't worry! You can go back in time and revert the game with *Version History*!

Section 1 Clause 2: How to Create Game Passes

Game Passes are purchasable items that allow a player to receive special in-game benefits.

To create a pass, you're going to want to go to the official page for your game on the Roblox website. Then, Scroll down a bit and hit the *Store* tab. You should then section pictured below.

Select *Add Pass*.

Next, you should be greeted the Game Pass editor screen. Here, you can upload your Game Pass image, write a name, and write a description.

You'll notice that at the top right, there's link that says *Click here* that brings you to a complete tutorial for Game Passes. Please use that tutorial if you have any problems with creating your Game Pass.

To make your Game Pass, fill in all the info needed, such as the description and the name. You cannot create a Game Pass without an image!

Once you've finished, select *Preview*. You'll be greeted with a screen displaying the options that you've selected.

If all looks right, select *Verify Upload.*
You should then receive the following popup confirming that the Game Pass has been created

You've successfully created a Game Pass!

Be sure to search for Game Pass design tutorial videos online for a more professional look.

Section 1 Clause 3: How to Create Badges

Badges are much like Game Passes, except they're earnable items that players can achieve while playing your game, and cost 100 Robux each. Badges are publically displayed on players' profiles.

With a badge, you can either choose to lay it out in the map of your game somewhere, or you can script it to make players do specific things to earn the badge, such as meeting the owner of the game.
Remember, if you're SCRIPTING the badge has to be in the game somewhere players can't get to, so that they can't simply step on it to achieve. Usually, I put mine under the maps.

To create a badge, go to Develop > My Creations > Badges. Then, select which one of your games you want to be active in. Next, choose your badge image from your computer files. Then, give it a name and description and hit *Preview*. The image will take a few minutes to pend, but you're able to purchase the badge while it's pending.

Next, make sure that the game the badge is being posted to looks correct, and purchase the badge for 100 Robux.

Next, open the game you want the badge to be in using Roblox Studio.
Then, go to Toolbox and select the dropdown box and hit *My Models.*
Then, look for the badge you just bought and select it so that it appears in the game.

Once your badge has been inserted into the game, place it where you would like it.
Then, exit and Publish your game for other users to enjoy!

You've successfully created your badge and it is now able to be achieved by players that play your game!

Section 1 Clause 4: Opening Roblox Studio

To get started with Roblox Studio, of course, you will need to download Roblox Player and Roblox Studio. Both download together when you click the *Play* button on any Roblox game.

Upon its initial startup, Roblox Studio should look like as pictured below

Select *Baseplate* and allow a few moments for it to start up.

This is the screen you should be seeing throughout this book to fully follow along with each tutorial.

Good luck!

Section 2: Studio Basics

Section 2 Clause 1: Personalizing your Studio

Now that you're in studio, let's go over the basics.

Let's get your studio all set up and personalized to your liking.

Select the *View* tab at the top of your screen. Next, select *Properties*. Position it to wherever you would like.

Next, select *Explorer*. Again, position it to your liking.

Then, *ToolBox* and *Output*. Make sure everything is set up in a way that you can easily remember and master.

Section 2 Clause 2: Explorer

The *Explorer* window is one of several windows that we'll be using constantly. This is where you can access every single thing that you have added to your game. The Explorer contains several services, such as: *Workspace, Players, Lighting, ReplicatedFirst, ReplicatedStorage, ServerScriptService, ServerStorage, StarterGUI, StarterPack, StarterPlayer, SoundScape, Chat, LocalizationService, HttpService* and *InsertService*.

Explorer should look like this

Service	Function
Workspace	A container for all physical parts. Any part you can see and interact with when you play your game will be stored here.
Players	A container for all the players currently in the game.
Lighting	Responsible for all visual lighting effects.
ReplicatedFirst	When you join your game, the contents of ReplicatedFirst will load for you before any other part of the game does.
ReplicatedStorage	A container designed specifically for storage.
ServerScriptService	A container designed specifically for containing scripts.
ServerStorage	Similar to ReplicatedStorage, but its contents will only be accessible by the server (servers Vs. clients will be explained later).
StarterGui	Gives a copy of every GUI it contains to each player whenever they spawn.
StarterPack	Gives a copy of every tool it contains to each player whenever they spawn.
StarterPlayer	Responsible for giving the players new avatars whenever they spawn.
SoundScape	Responsible for all audio effects.

Chat	Responsible for running the default chat system.
LocalizationService	Responsible for automatic language translation.
HttpService	Can send messages to other websites.
InsertService	Can load assets from the Roblox website such as catalog items into your game.

There are actually many more services than this. The rest are not shown in the explorer because they are not designed to act as containers.

Note: Since the writing of this book, several services have been either changed or added. If something new has been added and it's not explained here, check out the API section of wiki.roblox.com/ and search for it.

Section 2 Clause 3: Client Vs. Server

This is something you're DEFINITELY going to need to know if you don't already. It's very simple, and it's something that you should understand fairly quickly.

The Server is the ENTIRE game. More specifically, the entire running server. Client, however, is ONLY a single player.

To make this a bit more understandable, here's an example.

If I make an object that spams the clients with bricks, only the clients will see the bricks on their screen. The bricks will be invisible to the server. The server won't crash, but the players will. However, if I spam bricks into the SERVER, the ENTIRE server will feel it, and eventually collapse.

Section 2 Clause 4: Adding Objects

The absolute most important thing you need to learn when creating games on Roblox is how to add in objects from the Insert Object menu.

To insert an object, let's say a *Script*, you're going to want to right-click the Workspace Explorer service. Then, select *Insert Object*. Next, select *Script*. An object entitled *Script* should have been entered into Workspace. This object is where we will be doing our coding throughout this book.

To open it, left-click it twice.

Scripts save when you close them, so you don't have to worry about saving them manually.

Section 2 Clause 5: Part Properties

A big part of getting to know Roblox is getting to know about *Properties*. If you don't already know what *Properties* are in Roblox, be sure to look for it on the *Definitions* page.

Every single object under Explorer has a property, but for this lesson we're going to check out a *Part*'s properties.

To get to the *Properties* pop-up, select the *View* tab at the top of your Roblox Studio screen, and then select *Properties*. The following contains every Part Property that you'll be using most often.

Group	Name	Description
Appearance	BrickColor	Color of your part
	Color	RGB color of your part
	Material	What your part's made of
	Reflectance	Shininess of your part
	Transparency	Part's see-through level
	----------------------------	----------------------------
Data	Name	Name of your part
	Parent	The object your part is inside of

	----------------------------	----------------------------
Behavior	Anchored	Whether or not your part is affected by Roblox physics
	Archivable	Whether or not your part can be cloned and saved
	CanCollide	Whether or not a player can walk through your part
	Locked	Whether or not your part can be selected in Studio
	----------------------------	----------------------------
Part	Shape	Shape of your part
	Size	Size of your part
	----------------------------	----------------------------
Surface	BackSurface	Surface connection type
	BottomSurface	Bottom connection type
	FrontSurface	Front connection type
	LeftSurface	Left connection type

	RightSurface	Right connection type
	TopSurface	Top connection type

Note: For the Surface data properties, I like to set them all to the Smooth setting. It gives the best look, and, unless you know what you're doing, the others won't make any sense in your projects.

Section 2 Clause 6: Team Create

Team Create is a Roblox Studio mode that allows you to create in-Studio projects with other Roblox players. To Start Team Create, select the *View* tab and choose Team Create.

Now that you've opened the Team Create popup, you might be greeted with a *Publish and enable Team Create to built this place together with your friends* screen.

If you get this screen, it's simply because the game you're currently in on Studio hasn't been published to the Roblox website. Simply select *Publish* and choose a place in which you would like to publish your game.

Now that your game is published, you should be greeted by this text. To start Team Create, simply hit *Turn ON*. You can turn this off at any time.

Now that Team Create is ON, you should see a screen showing who is currently online in the game on Team Create.

To add another user, simply time in their username under *Invite a friend*!
Once an invite is sent out, your friend will receive a message in their Roblox inbox stating that they've been invited to your Team Create server.

Note: User must be on your friends list in order for the invite to be able to be sent out.

For Team Creates in GROUPS, however, you would do pretty much the same thing you did here. However, instead of inviting the player, they'd have to have Studio abilities in your group.

Section 2 Clause 7: Output

The Output is a text box that gives the status on everything running in your game. You can send messages to Output by using a *print("")* command, as shown below.

```
part = script.Parent
wait(2)
print("Setting transparency to .5")
part.Transparency = .5
if part.Transparency == .5 then
    wait(2)
    part.Transparency = 0
    part.Reflectance = 1
end
print("Script completed")
```

Setting transparency to .5 and *Script completed* will now appear in Output.

When writing any script, you're going to want to use Output. It will tell you if there is a problem with a script if it detects it.

Section 2 Clause 8: UI Editor

When creating GUIs, the Roblox Studio-integrated *UI Editor* is your BEST friend!
It's located under the *Model* tab and looks like this

Now, let's get a GUI ready to be prepared. Insert a *ScreenGUI* into *StarterGUI*.
Next, enter a *Frame*, and a TextBox inside of that. If done correctly, that should look like this

StarterGui
>ScreenGui
>Frame
>TextBox

Now, select the *UI Editor* and click the *Frame* GUI on the screen.

Now that you have that selected, drag it to the middle of the screen (or wherever you want it) and resize it.

Now that you have it where you would like it, select the *TextBox* GUI and position it to where you would like it on the frame.

There are more properties you can change to really give your GUI(s) a nicer look. Keep playing around with them!

Section 3: Basic Commands

Section 3 Clause 1: Print

Print is a command that will let you send messages to your *Output*.

Every new script that you enter into your game starts with the *Print* function, *Print("Hello World")*. This line sends the message *Hello World* to Output. To shed more light on *Print* commands, here's a script that we found that uses them.

```
part = script.Parent
wait(2)
print("Setting transparency to .5")
part.Transparency = .5
if part.Transparency == .5 then
wait(2)
part.Reflectance = 1
part.Transparency = 0
end
print("Script has been completed")
```

The *print* commands are the complete lines in bold.

As you can see, we made the code print *Setting transparency to .5* and *script has been completed* to our Output.

Section 3 Clause 2: Instance.new

Instance.new("", game.Service) is a command you can use in a script to insert a new item from the *Insert Object* menu.

Let's do a breakdown on what *Instance.new("", game.Service)* actually means and does.

The *Instance.new* part tells the script to get a new instance. Between the quotation marks in the parenthesis is where we display which instance we want created. Let's say we want a *Part* to be created. We'd add in *("Part,.* Next, we have *game.Service.* We leave the *game* part as it is, but change *Service* to whatever service we want a *Part* to spawn in. I'll be doing Workspace. Our final code with this would look like this

> Instance.new("Part", game.Workspace)

Next, we have an Instance command being used to create a *Message*

> Instance.new("Message", game.Workspace)
> game.Workspace.Message.Text = "This is a message"

In the Instance command seen above, we can see that a *Message* is being created. Then, the *game.Workspace.Message.Text = "This is a message"* part makes the Message say *This is a message*.

Section 4: Variables & Data Types
Section 4 Clause 1: Variables

A *variable* is a name that you can use to hold a value.

To start making variables, you need to assign a *value* to the variable. You can name the variable anything you wish, just don't add spaces or special characters.

myVariable = "This is a variable"

This now sets *myVariable* to equal *The Value*

You can also set the value to different data types, such as *strings*, *numbers* and *booleans*. *Strings* are text values that belong between quotations. *Numbers*, of course, are number values that can be held. *Booleans* are *true* or *false* values.

stringVariable = "String"
numberVariable = 10
booleanVariable = **true**

We can then use the print function to show what these variables equal. Run the game, and look at the output

stringVariable = "String"
numberVariable = 10
booleanVariable = true

print(stringVariable) -- **String**
print(numberVariable) -- **10**
print(booleanVariable) -- **true**

Variables can be changed by assigning another value to them, as shown below

myVariable = "The variable"
myVariable = "The new variable"

print(myVariable) -- The new variable

Variables can also be used as a value, to assign *new* variables

myVariable = "The value"
myNewVariable = myVariable

print(**myNewVariable**) --The Value

http://bit.ly/2vH631i

Section 4 Clause 2: Data Types

Data Type	Definition	Example
String	Text data in quotations.	"This is a string"
Bool	True/False data.	true
Userdata	Hundreds of Userdata types.	Vector3
Nil	Has a value of nothing.	0

http://bit.ly/2wZoD8V

Section 5: Math Operators

Math Operators are symbols that indicate an operation (Addition, subtraction, multiplication, division etc.) and return a value.

Below, we can see an example of *Addition* being used in an Operator.

Local sum = 1+1
print(sum)

Sum is the total amount of two values that are added. In this case, we're using *1+1* which is equal to *2*. If we go ahead and run this code, we get the following:
Now, we can see that it printed *2*.

2

In the following table, you will see the Operators you can use in Lua, and what they do.

Operators	Their Function
+ (Addition)	1 + 1 = 2
- (Substraction)	10 - 1 = 9
/ (Division)	10 / 2 = 5
* (Multiplication)	10 * 2 = 20

Section 6: Conditionals, Logical Operators & Comparison Operators

Before we begin, let's go over the different types of Conditional statements.

if
else
elseif

Now, let's go over the operators

and	Conjunction of two items
or	One or the other

And now, let's put some of these statements to use

$$a = 5$$
$$b = 5$$

if a == 5 **and** b == 5 **then**
print(a+b)
end

Note: When comparing two things with coding, we'll be using two equal signs, rather than one, like when we're declaring and defining a Variable.

Now let's run the game and check Output.
If done correctly, the value *10* should be printed.

Now, let's throw in an *else*

```
a = 5
b = 5

if a == 5 and b == 5 then
    print(a+b)

else
print("Incorrect statement")
end
```

Now that you've thrown in an *else*, the string *Incorrect statement* if the either *a* or *b* don't equal *5*.

Now, let's replace the *else* statement with an *elseif*.

```
a = 5
b = 5

if a == 5 and b == 5 then
    print(a+b)

elseif b == 150 then
    print("b = 150")

end
```

Now with this, if you change *b = 5* to *b =150*, *b = 150* will be printed to Output.

Section 7: Scopes & Local Variables

Basically, *Local Variables* are almost the exact same things as *Variables (Section 4)*, besides one thing.

They can only work inside their *Scope*. *Scopes* are basically blocks of code such as *if true then*, *while true do*, etc.

```
If true then
local Var = 17
    print(Var)
end
```

With this line, the texts in bold are the *Scope*.

If we run the game and check Output, we can see that *17* is printed. However, if we were to place the Print command OUTSIDE the scope, we would receive *nil* in Output. This, as stated, is because a local will only work inside of its Scope.

However, we were to take out the *local* part of the Variable, it would become a global variable, and of course, would be able to be used throughout any part of the script following the variable's creation, as we can see below.

```
if true then
    Var = 17
  print(Var)
end

  print(Var)
```

With this, the value *17* will now be printed twice, as the variable now applies to the entire script, compared to the *Local Variable*, which only works, of course, locally.

http://bit.ly/2vwoqK7
http://bit.ly/2eJgTgK

Section 8: Manipulating Data Properties
Section 8 Clause 1: Changing BrickColor

Changing a Part's BrickColor is simple, and only requires a few lines of code.
Let's have a look at the code below and see what we can learn from it.

baseplate = game.Workspace.Baseplate

wait(2)
baseplate.**BrickColor** = **BrickColor**.new("Pink")

As we can see, the code starts with a *Variable*. It then moves on and waits two seconds
before running the line *baseplate.BrickColor = BrickColor.new("Ghost grey")*. This line
changes the color of the baseplate from what it was originally, to the color *Ghost Grey*.

Now, let's say you want to make the BrickColor change to a random color. Simply edit
the code to appear as shown below

Baseplate = game.Workspace.Baseplate

wait(2)
baseplate.**BrickColor** = **BrickColor**:Random()

The code for changing the color now reads *baseplate.BrickColor =
BrickColor:Random()*, which as stated previously changes the BrickColor to a random
color.

Section 9: Loops

Section 9 Clause 1: While Loops

While Loops are a bit of code that can be written to execute repeatedly.

For this demonstration, I will be making a Part's transparency go from .3 to .7 repeatedly.

First, enter a Part into your game (*Model* tab > *Part*). Then, right-click it in Explorer under *Workspace* and select *Insert Object*, then select *Script*.

Open the script, then enter the following bit of code

Part = game.Workspace.Part

This code tells the script what Part means

Then, hit the *Enter* key twice type in *while true do*, as shown below.

while true do

Next, hit the *Enter* key and *end* should appear two lines under. If not, simply write it yourself.

Between *while true do* and *end* is where the code that you want repeated to go. Remember, you must add *wait(WaitTimeHere)* after the script that you want repeated to go, so that it will not crash your computer. I will be using *wait(1)*, so that the transparency will change every second.

My code will look as shown below

```
Part = game.Workspace.Part
while true do
Part.Transparency = .3
wait(1)
Part.Transparency = .7
wait(1)
end
```

With that bit of code being repeated, it will repeatedly change the transparency of the Part.
Another way to use a While Loop is to have it activate when it meets a certain condition.

For example, let's set a part's transparency to .5. We'll enter the code
game.Workspace.Part.Transparency = .5. -- Make sure a Part is inserted into your baseplate.

Now, let's start with our loop.

Let's add a part every second ONLY if Part's transparency is *.5*.

We'll type the following into our script

```
while game.Workspace.Part.Transparency == .5 do
wait(1)
Instance.new("Part", game.Workspace)
end
```

If done correctly, your code should look as shown below

```
game.Workspace.Part.Transparency = .5
while game.Workspace.Part.Transparency = .5 do
    wait(1)
    Instance.new("Part", game.Workspace)
end
```

The code will check the transparency and see if it's .5.
If it is, a part will be added every second for the rest of time.

You can also try throwing in an *If Statement*!

Section 9 Clause 2: For Loops

For Loops are easy to begin learning. Basically, they're for countdowns. However, you can apply them to other aspects of your games.

Here's an example of a For Loop in a code

```
Message = instance.New("Part", game.Workspace)

For i = num, num, num do
Message.Text = "Intermission: "..i
wait(1)
end
```

Now, for the num, num, num part.

These numbers are for addressing how long your countdown is.

For example, I could use 20, 0, -1 to countdown *20 seconds*. The *0* part is how far you want the game to countdown to. Of course, I want *20* to countdown to *0*, so I did *20, 0*. Now, the *-1* part. This is how much you want your countdown to go by. For example, if I wanted it to go down by 10, I'd do *-10*.

You can also make the count go *up* by doing something like *0, 500, 25*.
This will make your script count from *0* to *500* by *25*s

Now, back to the code. Again, let's make it countdown 20 seconds to zero by changing *num, num, num* to *20, 0, -1*, as shown below

```
Message = instance.new("Part", game.Workspace)

For i = 20, 0, -1 do
Message.Text = "Intermission: "..i
wait(1)
end
```

Make sure to use wait(1) at the end of your For Loops, or else it would go from 20 to 0 immediately.

http://bit.ly/2wpXkSl

Section 10: Functions

Section 10 Clause 1: Functions

A *Function* is a group of code that can be executed with a simple one-word-phrase, but with the added *()* at the end. It can hold as many lines of code as you want to add to it.

To start your function, enter the following code

```
function namehere() --namehere() is the name of the function
```

Once you've typed in this line, hit the *Enter* key.
The code *end* should appear two lines below it. If not, simply add it yourself.

You've successfully started your Function's definition. Now, you need to decide what the function does. I want it to print the text *function,* so in between function *namehere()* and *end*, I'm going to type in *print("function")*, as seen in the picture below.

```
function namehere() --namehere() is the name of the function
print("Function")  --the job that the function has to carry out
end --tells the script that the function is done
```

We've now defined the function *namehere()*.To make the Function work, you'll want to hit enter twice under *end*. Then, type your function's name with the two parenthesis. My function's name is *namehere()*, so I'll type that in. You can also choose to make the function wait 2 seconds before executing by adding wait(2) right above your function's name, as shown below.

```
wait(2) --tells the script to wait two seconds
namehere() --tells the script to execute the function namehere()
```

Your entire script should look as shown below.

```
function namehere() --namehere() is the name of the function
print("Function") --the job that the function has to carry out
end --tells the script that the function is done
wait(2) --tells the script to wait two seconds
namehere() --tells the script to execute the function namehere()
```

Next, run your game (*Test* > *Play* dropdown arrow > *Run)*

If you did what I did and made the function print *function*, you should notice that Output prints it.

You've successfully created a function!

Section 11: Methods

Below is a list of some of the most important methods

Methods	What they do	Example of use
:Remove()	Removes item.	Part:Remove()
:Destroy()	Completely removes item and all memory to it.	Part:Destroy()
:Clone()	Clones an item.	Part:Clone()
:FindFirstChild()	Finds object by ClassName.	Local Player = script.Parent:findFirstChild("Humanoid")
:GetChildren()	Grabs children of item.	**for** *InsertServiceHere*, child **in** pairs(script.Parent:GetChildren()) **do**
:MakeJoints	Goes through all parts contained in a model. If any part's surface has a SurfaceType that can make a joint, it will create a joint.	script.Parent:MakeJoints()
:BreakJoints	Removes joint between objects.	script.Parent:BreakJoints()
:GetMass	Returns the object's mass; Differs depending on size/surface of the item.	script.Parent:GetMass()
:MoveTo	Moves item to new location	Part:MoveTo(Vector3, new(43, 32, 83))

Section 11 Clause 1: :Remove(), :Destroy() & :Clone()

:Remove() is a method to use in a script when you would like something to be removed. *:Destroy()* is a method to use if you want your script to COMPLETELY remove and destroy all traces of something in a script.

You'll want to make *:Remove()* your primary method for removing items in your scripts.

Below, we can see a :Remove() method being used in a script

```
Instance.new("Part", game.Workspace)
Part = game.Workspace.Part

wait(2)
Part:Remove()
```

Next, we see a :Destroy() method being used in the same script

```
Instance.new("Part", game.Workspace)
Part = game.Workspace.Part

wait(2)
Part:Remove()
```

Finally, we have *:Clone()*.
:Clone(), given in its name, is a method that clones (or duplicates) an object.

Here's basically same script from :Remove() and :Destroy() using :Clone()

```
Instance.new("Part", game.Workspace)
Part = game.Workspace.Part
wait(2)
Part:Clone().Parent = game.Workspace
```

The *.Parent = game.Workspace* part of the code tells the script to make the cloned *Part* a *child* of *Workspace*.

Section 12: Events

Basically, *Events* are, of course, events that are activated when a certain trigger is met. For example: Touching a part, player joining, etc.

Before we start going over *Events*, it's important that you know how to find them to see which events you can use with specific objects and/or items.

First, go to the *View* tab in studio, and then select *Object Browser*

The events are marked with lightning bolt icons.

To get the drift of events, we're going to write a code that displays a message letting the server know that a player has entered the game.

This will be a *PlayerAdded* event.

```
game.Players.PlayerAdded:Connect(function(player)) --1
Instance.new("Message", game.Workspace) --2
game.Workspace.Message.Text = "Player "..player.Name.." has joined the game!" --3
wait(2) --4
game.Workspace.Message:Remove() --5
```

#1 is the event itself
#2 inserts a *Message* into the game
#3 makes the Message's text say *Player ***Usernamehere*** has joined the game!*
#4 makes the game wait two seconds
#5 removes the message from the game

http://bit.ly/2vLWFbM

Section 13: Tables

Before we begin with Tables, it's vital to understand that a *Table* is also referred to as an *Array*, which stores values inside.

local myTable = {"This", "Is", "My", "Table"}

For example:

In order to make a table variable, you need to add the *{}* symbols after the = sign, as shown above. To separate values, you're going to put the value itself inside the "" symbols, with a comma separating them.

A table has positions for every value inside the table.
For example:

Value	Number in Table
This	1
Is	2
My	3
Table	4

And in order to retrieve a value from a table, you just do *TableName[PositionInTable]*
Example:

local Is = myTable[2]

You can also insert and remove items in a table, as shown in the functions below

Adding a new value:

table.insert(myTable, "Another")

Adds another table with the value *Another. MyTable* represents the table itself.

Removing a value:

table.remove(myTable, 4)

Removes the value located at position *4. MyTable*, again, represents the table itself.

table.sort(Table) is a function that can be used to sort a table. Lists the values from smallest to largest.

http://bit.ly/2gkTK41

Section 14: Positioning Parts with CFrame

CFrame, basically, is for positioning objects. In this lesson, we will be using CFrame in code. To start a CFrame, we need to get the position we want the object to be moved to. This is simple. Simply place a part where you want your object to be moved, and copy the part's position in *Properties*.

Now, let's start with the CFrame's coding. First, let's create two different Parts. Then, name them *Part1* and *Part2*. *Part1* will be moving to *Part2*'s position in this lesson. Put Part2 where you would like Part1 to be moved to, then open its *Properties* and copy its *Position*. For me, *Part2*'s position is *44.6, 0.5, 30.2*. Copy that and hold onto it for later.

Next, insert a *Script* into *Part1*.
Start off your script with *Part1 = game.Workspace.Part1* at the very top.

Then, hit the *Enter* key twice and enter *wait(3)* so that Part1 will wait 3 seconds before being moved.

CFrame's code looks like *game.Workspace.ObjectName.CFrame = CFrame.new(X, Y, Z)*.

Now, for *ObjectName*. This is where we enter the name of the Object we want moved. I would replace it with Part1, but since I already defined it at the top of the script, I can cut the CFrame code down to Part1.CFrame = CFrame.new(X, Y, Z)

CFrame works with the X, Y, Z axis for positioning, so that's what the *(X, Y, Z)* is.

Now that we have that down, we need to enter the position that we want Part1 to be moved to in the *(X, Y, Z)* area. As stated earlier, I want my Part to travel to the position *44.6, 0.5, 30.2*. I'll change *(X, Y, Z)* to *(44.6, 0.5, 30.2)*. Our CFrame code should now look like *Part1.CFrame = CFrame.new(44.6, 0.5, 30.2)*

If done correctly, our entire script should now look like this (Besides the position. Yours will likely be different). View the following page for the completed code.

```
part = script.Parent

wait(3)
part.CFrame = CFrame.new(44.6, 0.5, 30.2)
```

Section 15: String Manipulation

A string is always inserted into two quotation marks. One at the beginning of the string itself, and one at the end.

Example:

MyString = "This is a string"

Since we know that, we can move on to manipulating them! Look in the table below, for their names, descriptions and examples on how to use them!

Name of String	Description	Example Input	Output
string.byte()	This function returns ASCII values of the characters.	print(string.byte("KinqAndi")	>075 105 110 113 065 110 100 105
string.char()	Returns a string with the length equal to the number of arguments, in where the characters are ASCII representations equal to the corresponding number.	**print(string.char**(075, 105, 110, 113, 065, 110, 100, 105))	>KinqAndi
string.find()	Returns the position of the first match of	**print(string.find("KinqAndi", "Ki"))**	>1,2

		pattern in string.		
string.format()	Uses its first argument as a template, where the following arguments are added, and using the format string to change values to strings.	**print(string.format("letter 65 is %c", 65))**	>letter 65 is A
string.len()	Returns the amount of characters are found in a string.	**print(string.len("KinqAndi"))**	>8
string.lower()	Returns a string, lowercase from original.	**print(string.lower("KINQANDI"))**	>kinqandi
string.match()	Looks for the first match of a pattern in a string.	**print(string.match("Hope this book is useful", "t%w+"))**	>this
string.rep()	Returns a string where the string are combined a certain amount of times.	**print(string.rep("KinqAndi", 3))**	>KinqAndiKin qAndiKinqAn di
string.reverse()	Returns the string reversed.	**print(string.reverse("KinqAndi"))**	>idnAqniK
string.sub()	Returns the substring which starts at certain position, and ends at another.	**print(string.sub("KinqAndi", 1,4))**	>Kinq
string.upper()	Returns the string in Uppercase.	**print(string.upper("kinqandi"))**	>KINQANDI

string.gmatch()	Returns an iterator function which, whenever it is called, it returns the next captures from a pattern over a string.	S = "This is just a test" -- **Sentence** **for** w in string.gmatch(S,"%a+") **do** print(w) **end**	>This >is >just >a >test
string.gsub()	Returns a copy of string in which all (first number if given) occurrences of pattern have been replaced by a replacement string.	**S = "This is just a test"** **print(string.gsub(S, "This", "Dis"))**	>Dis is just a test

Section 16: More Roblox API

In order, to use *Web API*s, you have to use the functions of *HttpService*. But first, we need to enable *HttpEnabled*. First, select the *HttpService* Explorer service.

Then, in the *Properties* window, make sure HttpEnabled is checked off

HttpService (Explorer service) > Check off HttpService

After checking off the "HttpEnabled" property, we can now move on!

Now, you can access the HttpService by adding this code at the top of your script:

local HttpService = game:GetService("HttpService")

Functions	What it Does
:GenerateGUID(bool wrapInCurlyBraces)	Generates a globally unique identifier.
:JSONDecode(string input)	Decodes a JSON String into a lua Table.
:JSONEncode(Array input)	Encodes a lua Table into a JSON String.
:UrlEncode(string input)	Returns a string with all unsafe ASCII chars replaced by a % followed by two hexadecimal values.
:GetAsync(string url)	Sends a HTTP GET request to the given URL and returns the response body.
:SetAsync(string url, string data)	Sends a HTTP POST request to the given URL.

First, we have to get the date off the website, for example let's say we are trying to receive data from this API:

https://www.roblox.com/UserCheck/DoesUsernameExist?username=KinqAndi

This tells us if a username is available for use.

We can then do the following:

```
URL = "https://www.roblox.com/UserCheck/DoesUsernameExist?username=KinqAndi"
    local Body = HttpService:GetAsync(URL)
    local myLuaTable = HttpService:JSONDecode(Body)
```

Now since, we have the lua table, we can see if the username is already in use, by doing the following.

```
if myLuaTable.success == true then
    print("Username is in use!")
else
    print("Username is not in use!")
end
```

Section 17: DataStores

Stats

Key	Value
Cash_37474696	666
Name_37474696	"KinqAndi"

As you can see in the table above, there is a *Key* and Value called. For each datastore, you can set and get the values of the keys.

First of all, let's look at some methods we can use with DataStores in the table below!

:GetAsync(s)	This would retrieve the value of the key "s"
:SetAsync(s, Value)	This would set the Value of the key "s" to the "Value" argument
:IncrementAsync(s, 1)	This would increment the value of the key s by 1

First what we need to do is store the DataStore in a variable such as this:

local DataStore = game:GetService("DataStoreService"):GetDataStore("Stats)

Retrieving the Value:

$$\text{print(DataStore:GetAsync(``Cash\_37474696''))}$$

>**666**

Setting the Value:

$$\text{DataStore:SetAsync(``Cash\_37474696'', 60)}$$

Since we just set the value is set to *60* and if we try to retrieve it again, it will say *60* instead of *666*

Incrementing the Value
*Note: This method **only** works **with Integers.***

$$\text{DataStore:IncrementAsync(``Cash\_37474696'', 1)}$$

Since the previous value was *60*, and we just incremented the value by *1*, it will now say *61* instead of *60*. We can use these two methods for loading and saving data in your game.

For example, we can use the *:GetAsync()* method to load the data, and *:SetAsync()* method to save the data!

Section 18: Advanced Functions

Built-In Functions	Description
math.abs(x)	Returns the absolute value of x
math.acos(x)	Returns the arccosine of x
math.asin(x)	Returns the arcsine of x
math.atan(x)	Returns the arctangent of x
math.atan2(y, x)	Returns the arctangent of y/x in radians
math.ceil(x)	Returns the smallest integer larger than or equal to x
math.sqrt(x)	Returns the square root of x
math.sin(x)	Returns the Sine of x
math.tan(x)	Returns the Tangent of x
math.cos(x)	Returns the Cosine of x
math.random(x,y)	Returns a random integer from the minimum and maximum values given (x,y)
math.rad(x)	Returns the Angle in Degrees x to Radians.
math.deg(x)	Returns the Angle in Radians x to Degrees.
math.log(x)	Returns the natural logarithm of x

There are more built-in functions, however, the most vital and important ones have been listed above.

http://bit.ly/2wpFQVR

Section 19: Running Codes In-Game Via Developer Console

Another big thing you'll be needing to know about is the in-game Developer Console, and how to run codes in-game with it.

Remember, to activate the FULL console, you've got to be either A) Owner of the game, or B) Owner/high rank of the group that the game is in.

If you're on a computer, press the *F9* key to open the console.
If you're on mobile, simply chat */console* into your chat.

After you've got the console open, you'll see a list of tons of different outputs and commands. Errors are highlighted in red, and sometimes orange.

To run codes using this console, you'll want to select the *Server Log* tab. Then, at the bottom, you'll see a bar with the text *Type command here*. This is where you'll be typing your codes.

To enter in the code, you'll want to hit the *Enter* key.

Below are some example codes to insert into the game.

Kill player
game.Workspace.PlayerNameHere.Humanoid.Health = 0

Insert brick
Insert.new("Part", game.Workspace)

Thanks for reading!

You may have finished the book, but learning the uses of Lua programming on Roblox is far from over. Be sure to constantly check the Roblox Wiki for tutorials on any new coding aspects added. New APIs are added daily.

Be sure to check for the next book in our series, *Roblox Lua: Programming Weapons*, if you're interested in learning how to craft your very own weapons from code!

This book is designed to be your push to learning Lua, and we hope we did a good job with getting you started. Make sure to do more research on every topic provided here so that you can expand your Lua skillset.

Be sure to use YouTube as another source for getting into more advanced stuff!

Be sure to also check out our Twitters!

Shane Merchant - www.twitter.com/merchantVlll
Andi Muhaxheri - www.twitter.com/kinqandirbx

Citations

Roblox - https://www.roblox.com/

Lua - https://www.lua.org/

AlvinBLOX - https://www.youtube.com/channel/UCp1R0TBvgM7gj0rwTYULmSA

Peaspod - https://www.youtube.com/user/PeasFactory

Basic ROBLOX Lua Programming by **Brandon LaRouche** -
https://www.amazon.com/Basic-ROBLOX-Lua-Programming-Black/dp/1475026048/ref=sr_1_1?
ie=UTF8&qid=1504320604&sr=8-1&keywords=roblox+coding

Zyleth - https://twitter.com/ZylethRBLX

Printed in Great Britain
by Amazon